Grammaropolis PRESENTS

Benny the Adverb

Written by Coert Voorhees
Illustrations by Powerhouse Animation

Meet the Parts of Speech

I name a specific person, place, thing, or idea. It's a big responsibility, naming things— a responsibility that requires a certain attention to detail.

Nelson the Noun

Some people say I'm all over the place. Some people call me a ball of energy. I take that as a compliment, because I just like to go, go, go!

Vinny the Action Verb

I take the place of one or more Nouns or Pronouns. I always want the Noun's job, and I hang out with the Verb and Adjective.

Roger the Pronoun

I'm perfectly happy to link Nouns and Pronouns with the appropriate Adjectives, but it's not like I'm going to expend a lot of energy doing so.

Lucy the Linking Verb

I modify a Noun or Pronoun. I tell what kind, which one, how many, or how much. I pride myself on being the most artistic of the parts of speech.

Jake the Adjective

Gather 'round everybody and let's have ourselves a wonderful time. I just love bringing words and groups of words together, don't you?

Connie the Conjunction

I modify a Verb, Adjective, or other Adverb. I tell how, when, where, to what extent, and under what condition. I often end in –ly, but I don't have to.

Benny the Adverb

I express emotion!! Yep, I'm always here, always ready with my commas and exclamation points, just in case.

Izzy the Interjection

They call me Preposition because I'm pre-positioned. I'm first. At the front. Before every other word in the phrase? Got it?

Lil Pete the Preposition

I am a chameleon. A spy. An undercover operative. I infiltrate the sentence and act as whatever part of speech suits me.

Slang

BENNY THE ADVERB

© 2019 Grammaropolis

Graphic Design by Mckee Frazior
Printed by Friesens, Altona, Manitoba, Canada

Text and Illustrations © 2011 by Grammaropolis LLC

This book is typeset in Komika Text

Distributed throughout the world
by Ingram Publisher Services
www.ingrambook.com

Printed in Canada

Benny the adverb loved to modify verbs, adjectives, and other adverbs.

1

Occasionally, he even disagreed with other adverbs.

This platypus is very cute.

I think it's hardly very cute at all.

5

Vinny tended to drive enthusiastically.

You must drive cautiously.

Jake was often afraid at the movies.
EXIT
This is scary!
We're actually okay.
It's not real.

And when his sister, Angelica, needed help deciding the extent of her own adverbs, Benny was there for her, too.

Then, with the help of Li'l Pete the preposition, Benny searched under the table.

Let's look inside the boxes, too.

My lock is here!

16

Connie the conjunction came over to help.

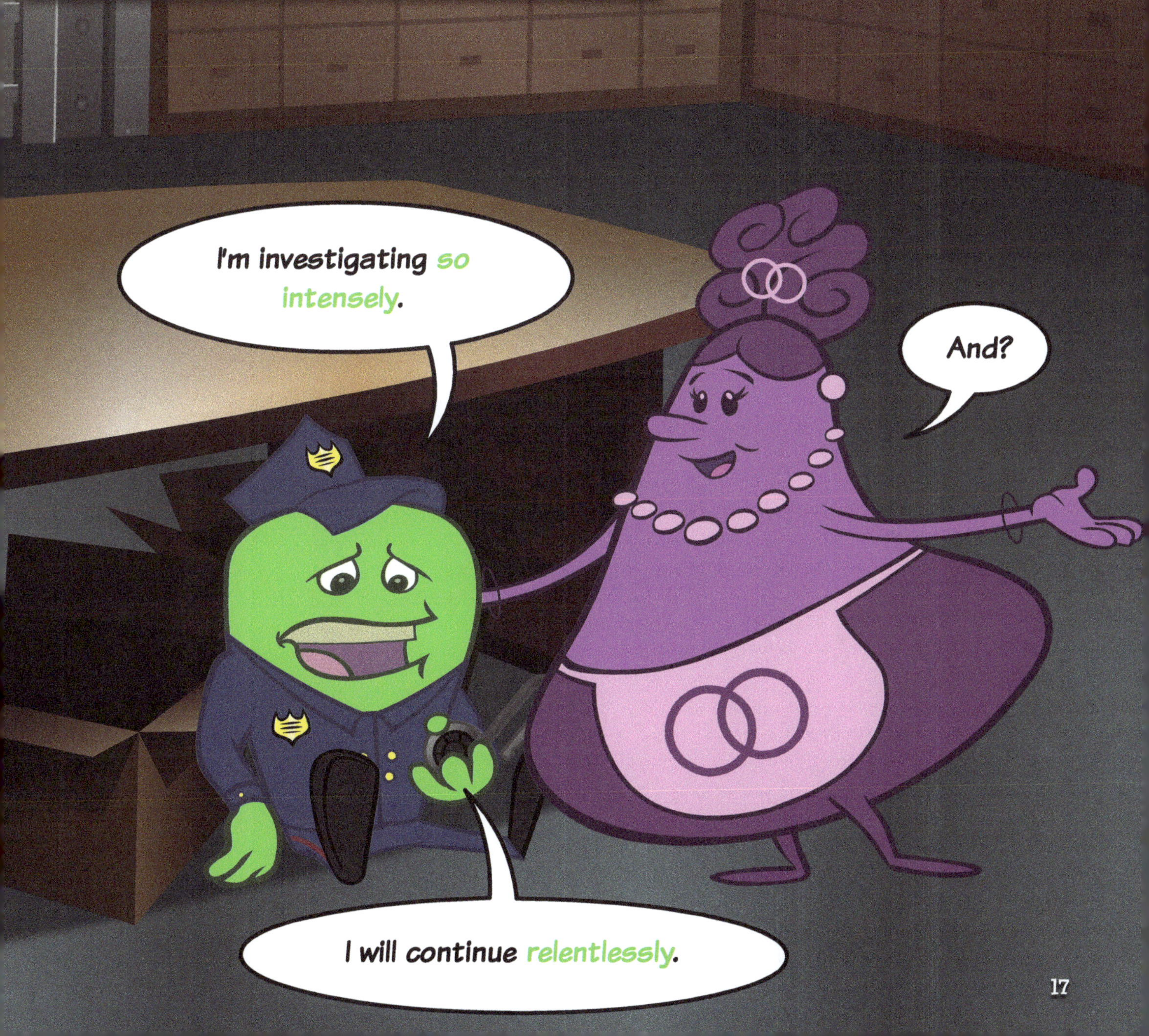

Then Angelica chipped in with a comparative adverb of her own.

Let's look harder.

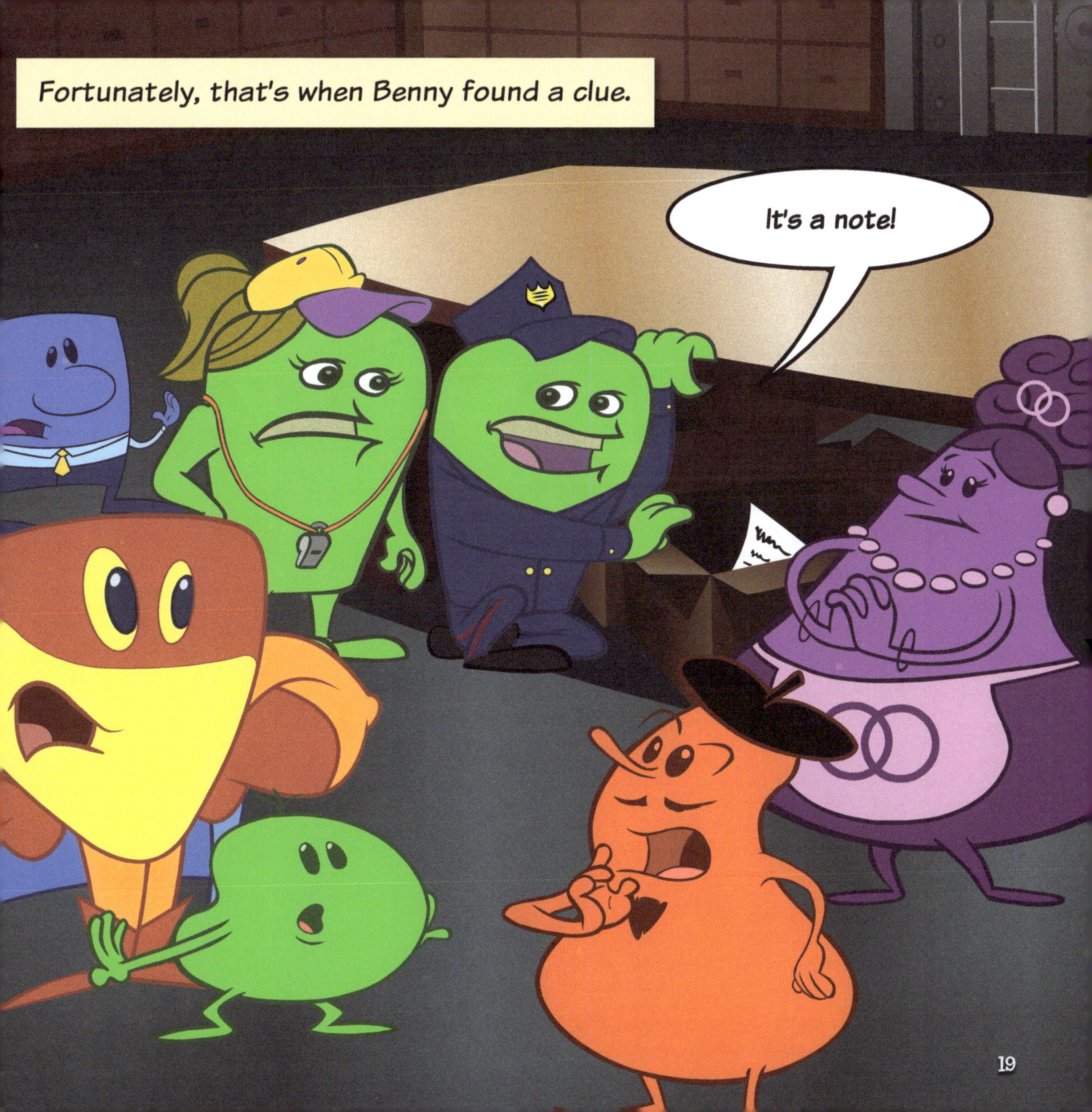
Fortunately, that's when Benny found a clue.
It's a note!

Benny had been so focused on giving adverbs to others, he'd forgotten to save some for himself.

Modifications:
Verbs, Adjectives,
& Adverbs

ADVERBS

An adverb modifies a verb, adjective, or other adverb.

I usually end in -ly, but I don't have to.

MODIFYING A VERB

Speak softly and carry a big stick.

MODIFYING AN ADJECTIVE

My classmates are incredibly silly.

MODIFYING ANOTHER ADVERB

Hector left the haunted house screaming quite loudly.

HOW

An adverb tells how.

The fire spread quickly.

I landed awkwardly when I fell off the trampoline.

EXAMPLES

quickly
awkwardly

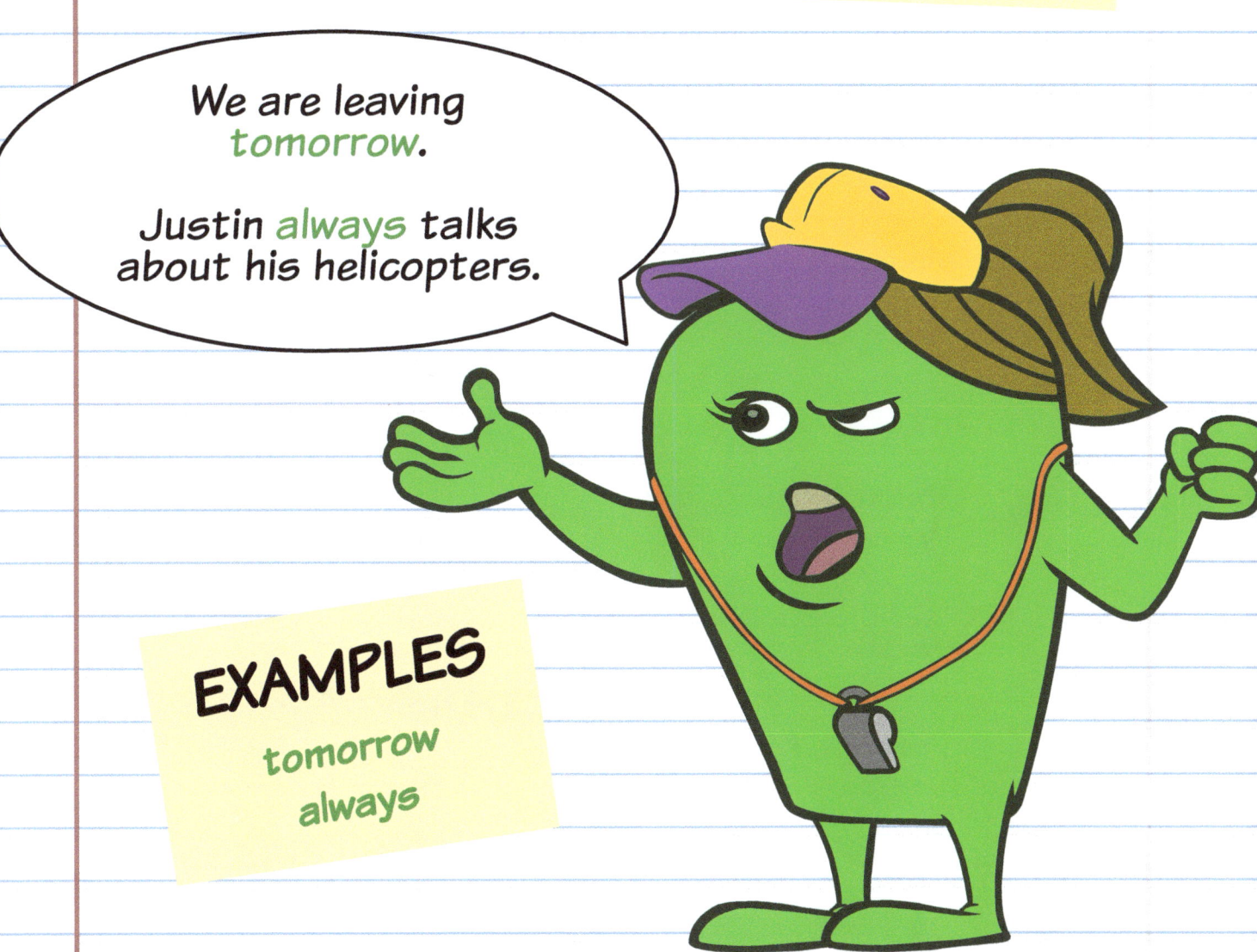

WHERE

An adverb tells where.

My best friend lives nearby.

Please go there and give Maria all of your dinosaurs.

EXAMPLES

nearby

there

TO WHAT EXTENT

An adverb tells to what extent.

> Susan emptied her locker completely.
>
> I hardly touched my chickpea mousse!

EXAMPLES

completely

hardly

ADVERB CLAUSE

An adverb clause is used to indicate under what condition something will take place.

We will win the game if we try hard.

Unless she studies, Suzie will fail the test.

EXAMPLES

if we try hard
Unless she studies

COMPARATIVE ADVERBS

A comparative adverb is used when making a comparison between people, places, or things.

She runs faster at school than at soccer practice.

Franklin does his homework less carefully than his sister does.

EXAMPLES

faster

less

SUPERLATIVE ADVERBS

A superlative adverb indicates the extreme quality of something. It is used when talking about three or more people, places, or things.

My teacher is the most helpful one in the school.

Out of everyone in my family, I eat beans the least frequently.

EXAMPLES

most
least

www.ingramcontent.com/pod-product-compliance
Lightning Source LLC
LaVergne TN
LVHW071213200326
834410LV00018B/572